VICTORIAN ILFRACOMBE

VICTORIAN ILFRACOMBE

Origins and Architecture of a North Devon Holiday Resort

Michael Laithwaite

DEVON BOOKS
Official Publisher to the Devon County Council

This book has been funded and produced by the Environment & Countryside Committee of Devon County Council. The County Engineer & Planning Officer is Edward Chorlton. The book was written by Michael Laithwaite on behalf of Devon County Council following his survey of the historic buildings of Ilfracombe in 1987 in preparation for a new list of buildings of special architectural or historic interest which is shortly to be issued by the Department of the Environment. This survey was funded by Devon County Council and North Devon District Council and the latter, together with the Ilfracombe Civic Society, have contributed towards the cost of publication of this book.

First Published in Great Britain in 1992 by Devon Books

British Library Cataloguing-in-Publication Data

Laithwaite, Michael
Victorian Ilfracombe: Origins and Architecture of a North Devon Holiday Resort
I. Title
720.942

ISBN 0 86114 874 6

Devon Books, 397 Topsham Road, EXETER EX2 6HD
0392 873215
and
Chinon Court, Lower Moor Way, Tiverton Business Park, Tiverton, Devon
0884 243242

Designed for Devon Books by Topics Visual Information
397 Topsham Road, Exeter EX2 6HD 0392 876800

Typeset by Exe Valley, Exeter
Printed and bound in Great Britain by Penwell Print Ltd, Callington, Cornwall

ACKNOWLEDGEMENTS
The publishers are grateful for the help given by Peter Thomas who provided the colour photographs, to Ian Maxted and the West Country Studies Library (WCSL) for provision of many of the Victorian Prints and photographs, and to the Devon Record Office.

CONTENTS

Ilfracombe today.

FOREWORD

'Ilfracombe' wrote John Betjeman 'is an epitome of seaside history'.* Certainly the short but decisive period in its long history, when it grew to its zenith as one of Victorian Britain's leading seaside resorts, has left us a legacy of classic nineteenth century seaside building. Ilfracombe is, with its terraces and villas, chapels and churches, shops and public buildings an epitome of the Victorian age, and one deserving of celebration, not least because it has survived to our own day virtually intact.

This book about the building of the Victorian town has emerged from a convergence of local and national partnerships concerned about Ilfracombe's future as much as its past. Its genesis was the commission of a major survey of the historic buildings in the town centre conservation area funded by Devon County Council and North Devon District Council. This promises much increased statutory protection for many historic buildings in the Victorian heart of Ilfracombe.

The survey had other important consequences. It prompted a lively debate about national standards for the listing of Victorian buildings and revealed an issue of importance to conservation strategy in general, that is the difficulty of recognising and protecting the coherence and completeness of a whole historic environment as opposed to its individual parts. What distinguishes Ilfracombe is not a

*Ilfracombe in: *First and Last Loves*, J. Betjeman, John Murray, 1952.

Gateway at the entrance to Westwell Hall, Torrs Park, designed by W. C. Oliver c. 1880.

claim about the architectural quality of its individual buildings (mostly modest against national criteria) but the consistency, architecturally speaking, of its Victorian personality. It is perhaps not too much to claim that the future of Ilfracombe will be a test of whether we can move from the protection of parts of the historic environment to the conservation of the whole.

I believe this book has a contribution to make to this wider debate. To understand how Victorian Ilfracombe was built is to emphasize the interweaving of social and economic history with architectural and building history. In their choice of Michael Laithwaite to undertake the historic buildings survey, the local authorities stimulated his diligent research into the riches of the nineteenth century archive material for the town, material which told a remarkably clear story about Ilfracombe's development. As a result Mr Laithwaite was commissioned to write this book.

I find the result compelling reading. The picture he paints is most illuminating about such matters as the design and planning of the developments, but it also gives us interesting portraits of the personalities and institutions of the period. For what is celebrated here is the achievement of a singular Victorian community in North Devon, of interest and importance to all involved in the conservation of our historic environment.

Peter Beacham
Inspector of Historic Buildings, English Heritage

The imposing Ilfracombe Hotel c. 1880. (Photo by John Stabb, courtesy WCSL).

—1— THE ORIGINS OF THE HOLIDAY RESORT

In 1794 the *Universal British Directory* described Ilfracombe in these terms: 'a populous, rich, trading, sea-port, especially with herrings, in the Bristol-channel; noted for maintaining coastal lights to direct the sailors; for its convenience of building and repairing ships; and for the safe shelter ships from Ireland find here, when it is extremely dangerous for them to run into the mouth of the Taw, which they call Barnstaple-water; and this is one reason why the Barnstaple merchants do so much of their business at this port ... It is a pleasant and convenient place for bathing, and much resorted to by the gentry for that purpose'.

In other words, Ilfracombe was to the outside world a predominantly commercial place, with only a sideline in the holiday trade. The directory's description, which draws heavily on Daniel Defoe's account of around seventy years before, in fact exaggerates even its commercial importance, for although it had been a borough with a weekly market, annual fair and seaport since the thirteenth century, it had never been one of the leading towns in the county. Its population in 1801 was only 1838, a thousand less than Bideford's and half that of Barnstaple. Its leading citizens, as shown in the directory, were a modest group: only two were classed as gentlemen, one of them a naval lieutenant and the other a surgeon and apothecary, while the eight most important tradesmen were a rope-maker, an anchor-smith, a grocer and corn-factor, two merchants and shipbuilders, a soap-boiler and tallow-chandler, an innholder and maltster, and a boat-builder and block-maker. Barnstaple and Bideford, by contrast, had 155 and 132 listed tradesmen respectively, as well as a substantial number of lawyers and medical men.

The holiday trade had been established in a modest way since at least 1771. On 26 July of that year the *Exeter Flying Post* recorded the arrival of six people (all women, five of them married) 'for the benefit of the air, salt-water and to spend part of the summer season'. Captain Fraine and his family were to arrive the next day. 'Capt. Vallacot, who spent some time here, intends to set off soon for Gibraltar, where his Regiment now is'. The article concluded: 'Of the very many persons who have frequented Ilfracomb [*sic*] for their health, during the summer season, for years past, but one has died; so salubrious is its air and waters'.

Clearly the town was on its way to becoming a fashionable watering-place. In this respect it was no innovator. Bath and Tunbridge Wells had been established as spas by the seventeenth century, while Scarborough and Brighton had started up as sea-bathing resorts in the 1730s. Among the Devon seaside resorts, however, it seems to have been one of the earliest, preceded only by Exmouth and Teignmouth. In 1788 the *Exeter Flying Post* was already praising 'the conveniency of the bathing machines' (Fig. 1), and by 1823 it was thought worthwhile to call in Welsh miners to cut a tunnel through the rocks to hitherto inaccessible beaches (Fig. 2). Indoor baths for invalids had been established at least a year prior to this, for they are mentioned in Lysons' *Magna Britannia* of 1822; in 1836 the splendid new hot and cold baths (the outside of which still exists) were added next to the entrance to the 'Tunnels Beaches', complete with a Greek Doric portico (Fig. 3).

Entertainments quickly followed: a regatta, fashionably attended, was established in 1828, and by 1830 there were 'Public Rooms' with a ballroom, reading and billiard-rooms. For those with more solitary tastes, the firm of John Banfield

FIG. 1
The Lady's Bathing Cove with bathing machines. This was one of the new bathing beaches made accessible in 1823. (From J. Banfield Scenery in the North of Devon, *Courtesy West Country Studies Library – WCSL).*

FIG. 2
The Tunnels made by Welsh miners opened up new bathing areas. (Photo by John Stabb, courtesy WCSL).

FIG. 3
The Bath House soon after its completion in 1836. The entrance to the Tunnels Beaches (which still survives) can be seen on the right. (From J. Banfield Scenery in the North of Devon, *courtesy Bideford Public Library).*

had established a lending library in 1823, followed in 1830 by a guidebook suggesting walks and expeditions in the neighbourhood.

Communicatons, too, had been improving. In the 1820s a new turnpike road was laid out between Barnstaple and Ilfracombe, and the harbour-pier, used by the packet-boats from Bristol and Swansea, extended and rebuilt.

Population rose sharply, doubling to 3679 between 1801 and 1841, and there was a parallel increase in the number of houses. Despite this, however, the town retained most of its medieval form, with new development limited mainly to the harbour end (Fig 4). In 1830 John Banfield described it as 'composed chiefly of one long street. Many of the principal lodgings, however, are to the east; where the extent and variety of view, added to the great increase of visitors to this favoured spot, has induced many to speculate in building.' He particularly mentioned Coronation and Montpelier Terraces; Hillsborough Terrace was added in the 1834 edition.

Banfield, however, was a local man who made much of his income from the visitors. E. D. Bourdillon, who came to the town as an outsider during his 'Three Weeks Tour in the Western Counties' in 1834, saw it in quite a different light. Ilfracombe, he wrote, 'does not justify the great idea many persons have formed of it'; it 'may become perhaps in time a nice watering place as some new houses have been built a short distance from the town which is in itself a dirty place with narrow streets &c.' Bourdillon was not usually a grumpy traveller, for he had praised all the South Devon resorts from Sidmouth to Torquay. Moreover, his view of the condition of the streets is supported by a reference in the *North Devon Journal* for 1831 to 'small pools of stagnant water, the heaps of rubbish and decayed vegetable matter in every stage of decomposition.'

In the late 1830s attempts were made to update the old centre of the town. Edwin Lammas's *Ilfracombe As It Is, or*

FIG. 4
A paddle steamer lies moored against the Old Quay Head in Ilfracombe Harbour c. 1849, before the building of the Promenade Pier. On the skyline are Hillsborough and Montpelier Terraces. (From a drawing by W. Spreat, courtesy WCSL).

the Strangers Guide wrote in 1840 of the 'principal street... much improved within the last two or three years by widening the carriage road, and by the erection of a number of handsome houses, with fashionable shop fronts. Many of the houses are elegantly furnished as lodgings.' Samuel Lewis's *Topographical Dictionary of England*, published in the same year, reported that: 'The excellence of the beach affords very great facilities for sea-bathing; several handsome lodging-houses have been opened, and the town is rapidly rising into reputation as a bathing-place.' In 1837 the town was lit by gas, only three years after Torquay and ahead of Teignmouth and Dawlish.

Yet A. B. Granville's *Spas of England and Principal Sea-Bathing Places*, published in 1841, completely ignored Ilfracombe, while discussing both Minehead and Weston-super-Mare on the Bristol Channel, and all the South Devon resorts from Exmouth to Torquay. *Blackwoods Edinburgh Magazine* for August 1856 described the town in the most scathing terms: 'Handsome the town of Ilfracombe is not... Overtopping the whole town in ugliness and pretension, no less than in altitude, are two terraces, which make two factory-like lines of building on the slope of the green hill... Except on those two unfortunate terraces, it gives itself no airs of fashion... It has no magnificent hotels.' Even Murray's *Handbook for Travellers in Devon and Cornwall* of 1859, though enthusiastic about Ilfracombe's coastline, is dismissive of it as 'this little watering-place'.

The truth is, perhaps, that Ilfracombe had been slow to develop by comparison with the South Devon resorts. Its accessibility by boat from Bristol and South Wales was poor compensation for being isolated from the railway system. The latter had already reached Teignmouth, Torquay and Dawlish in the late 1840s, whereas in North Devon even Barnstaple had to wait until 1854.

—2—
THE RISE OF THE LATE VICTORIAN TOWN

Ilfracombe's sanitary problems culminated in the cholera epidemic of 1849, followed in 1850 by a critical report from a Board of Health inspector. This resulted in the establishment the following year of the Local Board of Health (the predecessor of the Urban District Council). A new sewage works was completed in 1853; the water-supply was improved, and a new reservoir built in 1866. All this may seem rather commonplace detail, but it was important in building up the reputation of the resort. As late as the 1880s the Belgrave Hotel thought it sensible to print the slogan 'Sanitary Arrangements Perfect!' on its advertisement.

Not surprisingly, the 1840s and 1850s were a period of minimal growth for the town, both in population and in the number of houses. Visitors appear to have been more numerous, with lodging-house keepers (judging from the directories) up from twenty-two in 1844 to sixty-four in 1857, but the only substantial building development seems to have been the Hostle Park estate, begun in 1856. The real advance did not come until the 1860s with the establishment of the Ilfracombe Joint Stock Land and Investment, or Torrs Park, Company in 1860, followed by the Ilfracombe Hotel and Esplanade Company in 1863.

These two were major residential and hotel developments on a scale quite unlike anything that Ilfracombe had seen before. Both were begun in anticipation of the construction of the railway from Barnstaple, which was completed in 1874. Although the Ilfracombe Hotel was not finished until

1867 and the most impressive parts of Torrs Park were not built until the 1880s, the whole balance of the town began to change. Hitherto, its three hotels had been situated in the old streets: the Royal Clarence in the High Street, and the Royal Britannia and the Packet down by the harbour. Now a major hotel, capable of attracting wealthy foreigners such as Prince Frederick Willliam of Prussia and the Vanderbilts, was established on the seafront adjoining the fashionable bathing-beaches. It led the way to the development of Wilder Road as a centre for hotels and public entertainments.

Torrs Park had a similar effect in drawing the new residential areas over to the west end of the town. The early nineteenth-century terraces had nearly all been built at the east end above the harbour, where they had an extensive view of the Bristol Channel and the Welsh coast; the most westerly was Adelaide Terrace, which stood on the hillside above the High Street. Although the scenic qualities of the Torrs had been appreciated since the late eighteenth century, they had remained mostly a place for country walks. Morris's directory for 1870 shows how fashions had changed, with the gentry already moving to the first Torrs Park houses, and the terraces being let out as apartments. Torrs Park residents listed in the 1881 census return include two Indian Army officers, a major-general, a naval lieutenant, two retired merchants, a retired barrister and an accountant.

The effect of these developments can be judged from the 1872 edition of Murray's *Handbook for Travellers in Devon and Cornwall.* Whereas the 1859 edition had dismissed Ilfracombe as a 'little watering-place', the new edition was ecstatic about it: 'The new hotel, the many new terraces and villas, and the building which is everywhere in progress, indicate the increasing favour with which Ilfracombe is regarded by the crowd of autumn tourists. The railway in progress from Barnstaple will give increased facility for.

FIG. 5
The Promenade Pier c. 1904. Tied up left to right are the steamers Britannia, Westward Ho! *and* Bonnie Doon, *in the background the* Normandy. *(Courtesy WCSL).*

FIG. 6

Ropery Meadow, with bandstand and Victoria Pavilion (W. H. Gould, 1888). This remarkable photograph provides a vivid picture of Ilfracombe's tourist industry at the turn of the century. Groups of holidaymakers stroll in the sun on Capstone Hill, the pavilion is thronged and (right foreground) a music party prepares to entertain the crowds. (Photo John Stabb, courtesy WCSL).

reaching it; and it must be admitted that those who desire quiet and comparative solitude will do better to pitch their tents at Westward Ho or Lynton'.

Things were also changing in the harbour area, where the shipbuilding industry was in decline. The building of the Promenade Pier in 1873 enabled boats to dock at different stages of the tide (Fig. 5). The result was to encourage yet more boatloads of trippers from South Wales and to promote the east end of the town as a centre for mass tourism (Fig. 6).

Population rose sharply between the 1870s and 1890s to a total of 8557 in 1901, nearly five times the figure for 1801 and twice that for 1861. The number of houses rose at a similar rate, though here the increase was greatest in the 1880s. Lodging-houses rose from ninety-five in 1870 to 233 in 1889.

The seaside at Ilfracombe – against the background of the newly built town, Victorian holidaymakers are entertained by a Punch and Judy show.

—3—
THE TOWN PLAN

The physical growth of Ilfracombe is best illustrated by comparing the town plans of the 1840s with those of the 1880s. In 1840 the tithe map (Fig. 7) gives a vivid impression of what was still essentially the medieval town, consisting of a single street about a mile long (now Church Street, High Street and Fore Street) with deep, narrow building or 'burgage' plots at either side. Detached at the western end, on a spur of land flanked by the East and West Wilder Brooks, stood the medieval parish church.

Almost the whole of the street was lined with buildings, right down to the harbour, but little development had taken place elsewhere. A few houses had gone up on the roads leading out of the town, particularly along the Braunton (now St Brannock's) Road, Horne Lane and Portland Street, while the harbour area was beginning to spread westwards. Above the main street and Portland Street, the new Adelaide, Hillsborough and Montpelier Terraces stood in virtual isolation, with Coronation Terrace a little further down on the lower side of Portland Street. The slopes below the main street, facing the sea, were almost empty, apart from a villa here and there, although one plot had been developed as Regent Place with buildings on both sides. Northfield Road already existed as the link between the High Street and the Tunnels Baths, but with only a scatter of buildings set well back from the road-frontage. There were no buildings along the sea-front, except for the Baths.

Wilder Road was merely a lane, linked to the church by what is now Church Road, but not forking off, as at present, to Church Street.

The plan in Twiss & Sons' *Illustrated Guide to Ilfracombe and North Devon*, published about 1888 (Fig. 8), shows the dramatic growth of the town in the forty to fifty years since 1840. Below the main street the empty plots were now almost completely filled with buildings. Wilder Road had become a major thoroughfare and extended, probably in the 1870s, to link up with Church Street. On its seaward side, Runnacleave Road had been laid out in front of a group of villas (Runnamede House, Runnamede Villa and South Villas) erected in the 1840s. To the east, beyond the Ilfracombe Hotel, the town had acquired Ropery Meadow and laid it out as pleasure gardens in 1872; opposite them had been built in about 1880 the low two-storeyed row of shops that still exists (Fig. 9). The Victoria Pavilion (Figs 10 and 16), an indoor promenade and winter garden resembling a giant greenhouse, had just been built at the rear of Ropery Meadow, although too late to go on the plan.

The other main area of new development was to the west, where Torrs Park Road was now fully laid out (Plate 1). Building had started in the 1860s, with nine or ten of the houses occupied by 1870. Most of the houses, however, had been built only in the early 1880s and five in the middle of the north side, from The Torrs to Chartwood, were not yet in existence. They probably followed in about 1890; at least three are shown as occupied in Kelly's directory for 1893.

At the south-east end of Torrs Park Road a large triangle of ground, part of it known as Bloody Field after a Civil War battle of 1644, had also been built up in the early 1880s; here Brookdale Avenue and Church Road contained a more modest type of middle-class semi-detached house, whilst the Wilder Road side of the site had a long terrace of working-class and artisans' dwellings.

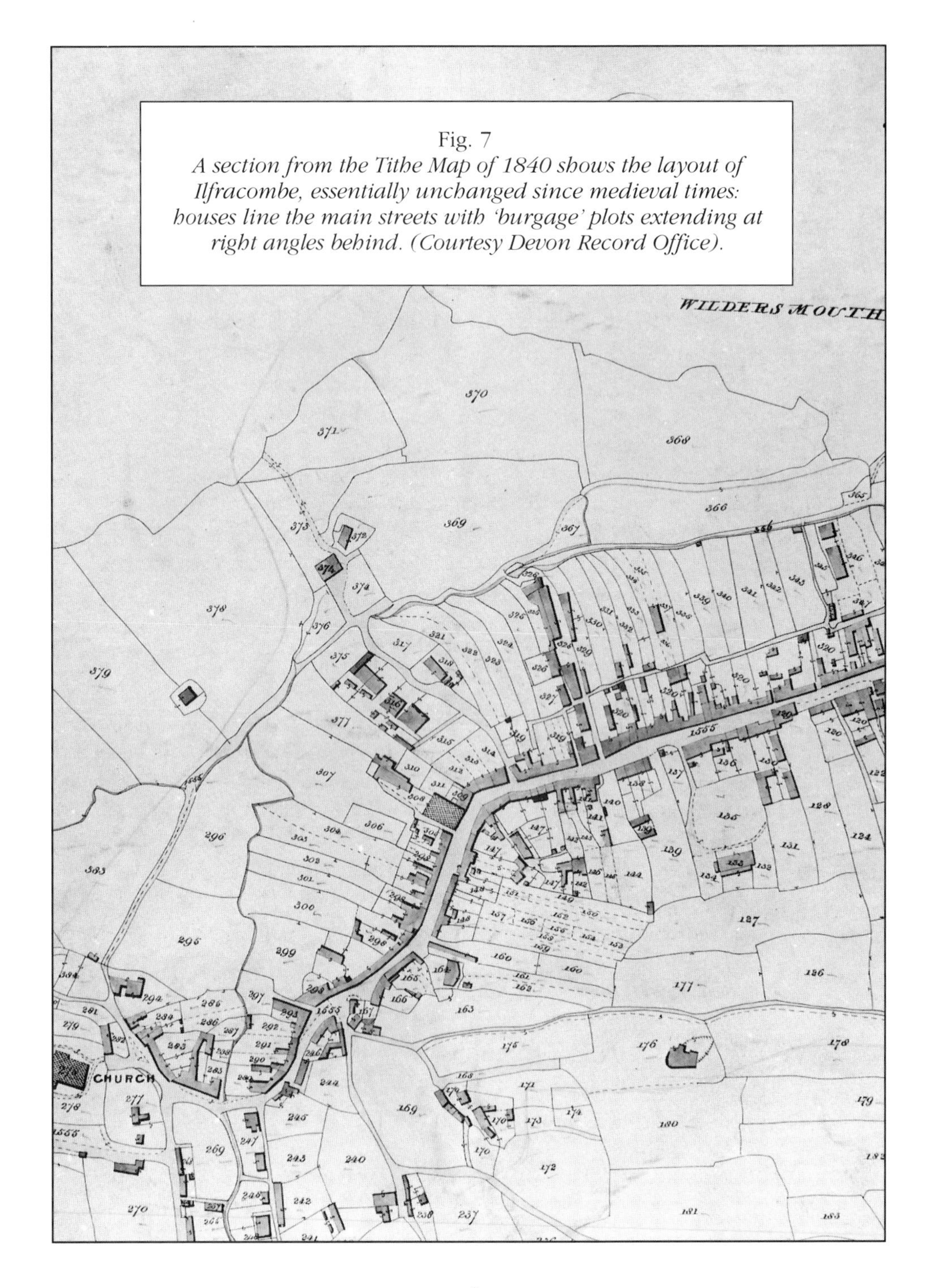

Fig. 7
A section from the Tithe Map of 1840 shows the layout of Ilfracombe, essentially unchanged since medieval times: houses line the main streets with 'burgage' plots extending at right angles behind. (Courtesy Devon Record Office).

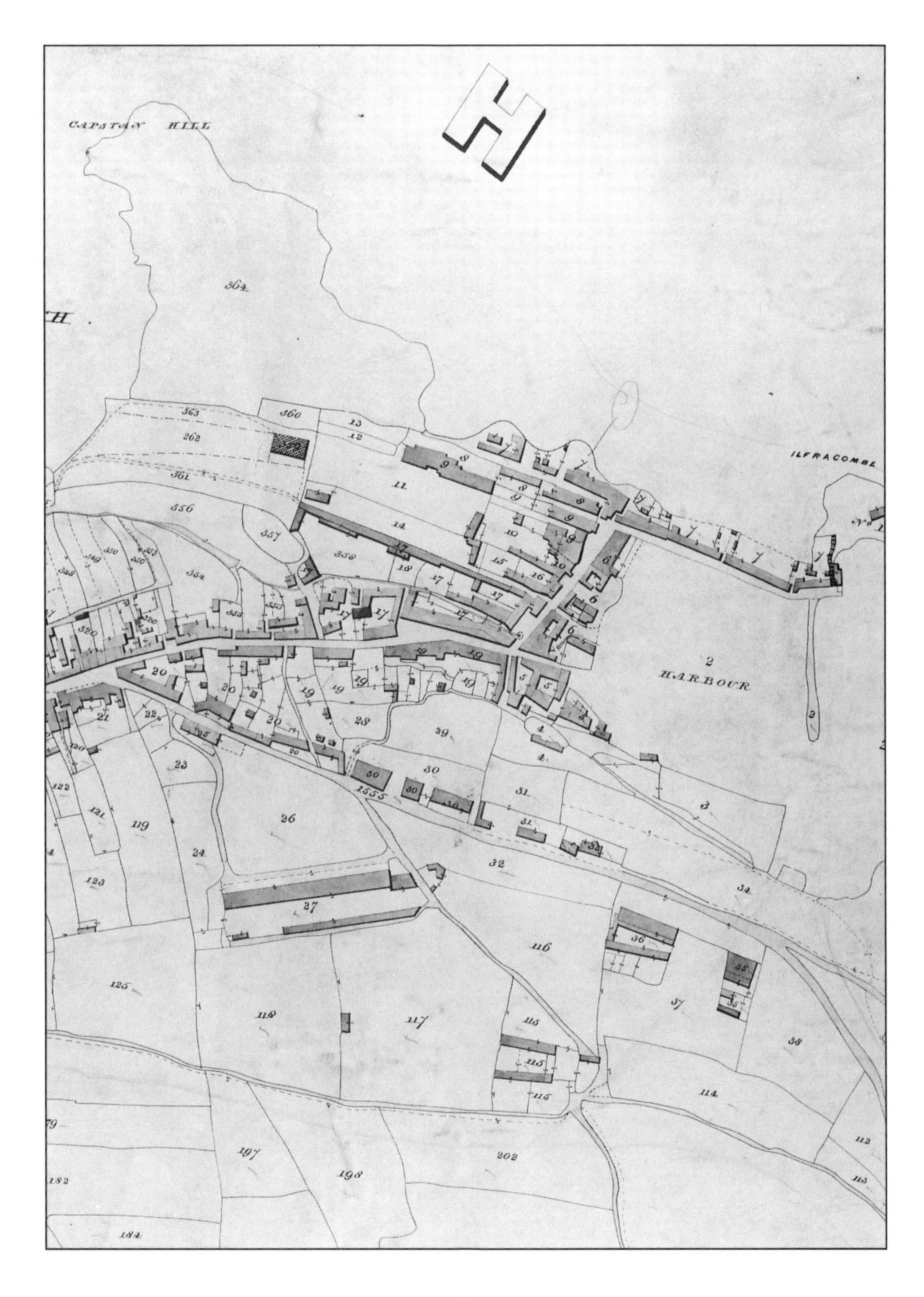
CAPSTAN HILL
ILFRACOMBE
HARBOUR

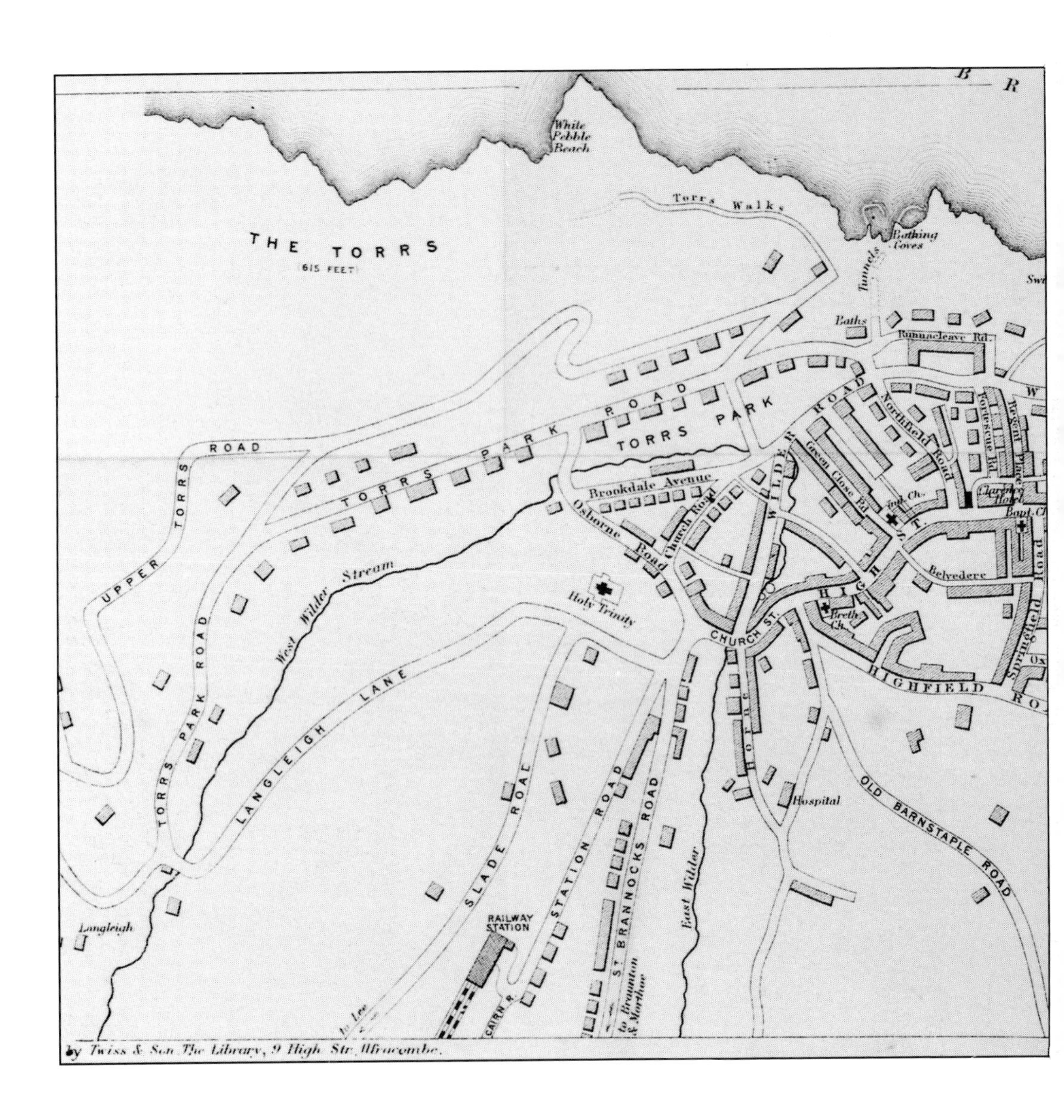
THE TORRS
(615 FEET)
White Pebble Beach
Torrs Walks
Bathing Coves
Tunnels
Baths
Runnacleave Rd.
TORRS PARK ROAD
TORRS PARK
TORRS ROAD
UPPER TORRS ROAD
Brookdale Avenue
Osborne Road
Church Road
WILDER ROAD
Green Close Rd
Northfield Road
Fortescue Rd
Regent Place
Belvedere
West Wilder Stream
Holy Trinity
CHURCH ST.
HIGH ST.
HIGHFIELD ROAD
Springfield Road
Horne
Hospital
OLD BARNSTAPLE ROAD
LANGLEIGH LANE
SLADE ROAD
STATION ROAD
ST BRANNOCKS ROAD
RAILWAY STATION
East Wilder
Langleigh
to Braunton & Mortho
to Lee
by Twiss & Son The Library, 9 High Str. Ilfracombe.

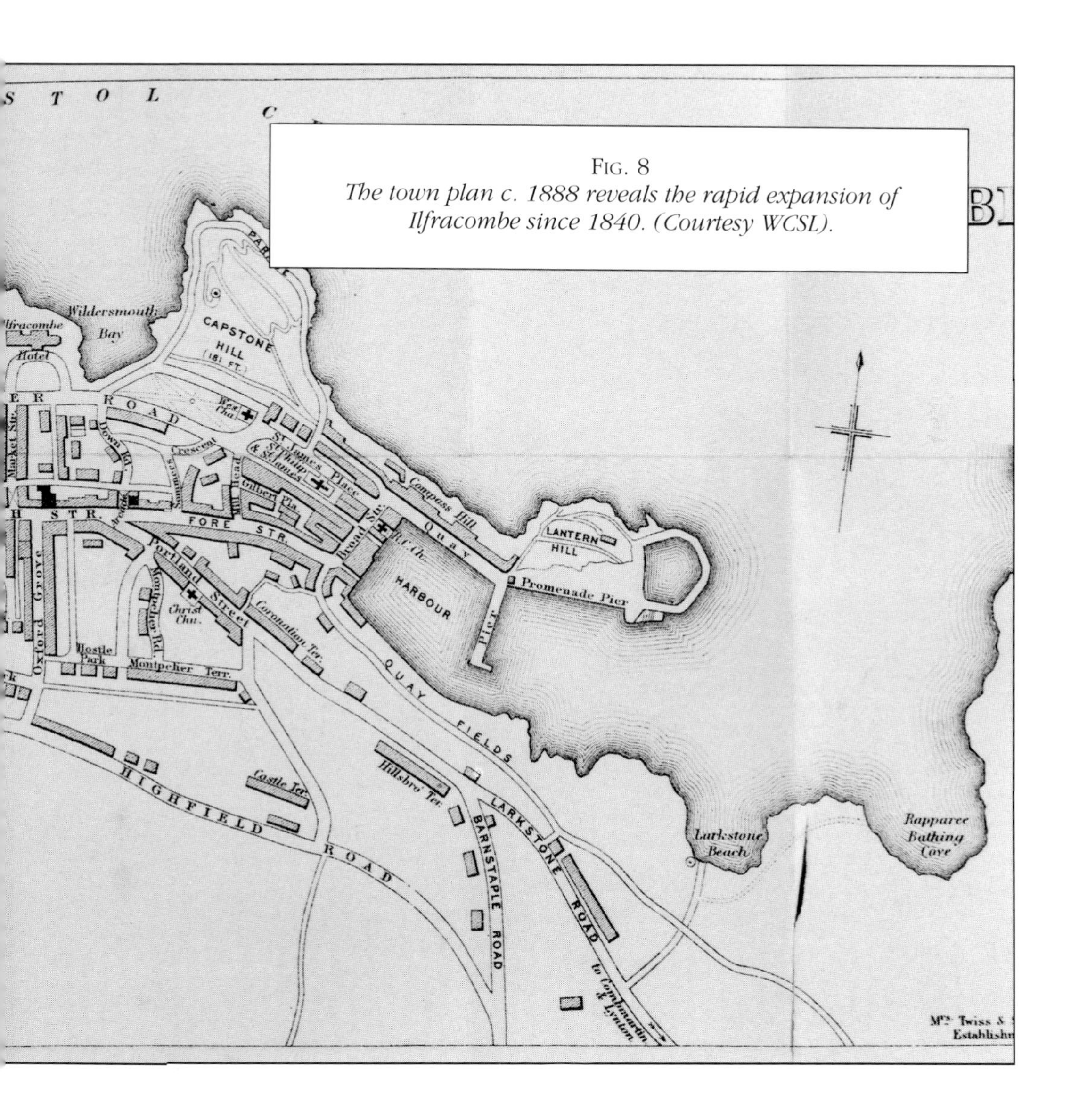

FIG. 8
The town plan c. 1888 reveals the rapid expansion of Ilfracombe since 1840. (Courtesy WCSL).

FIG. 9
Wildersmouth c. 1900. This was the original bathing beach before the Tunnels Beaches became accessible. On the right is the Ilfracombe Hotel and, facing the beach, Nos 1–8 The Promenade, a row of houses and shops by W. H. Gould, 1880. (Photo courtesy WCSL).

FIG. 10
The interior of the Victoria Pavilion c. 1898. The middle section was demolished in 1925 and replaced by a theatre, the end sections remaining until the 1960s. (Photo by John Stabb, courtesy WCSL).

Despite these developments, the parish church still retained much of its isolated aspect on the south side. The railway station had as yet engendered little building in its immediate vicinity. Slade (now Belmont) Road had several early and mid nineteenth-century villas and some more regular lines of buildings had grown up along Station Road and St Brannock's Road, but there were still long stretches of open frontage. Broad Park Avenue and the St Brannock's Park Estate were still to come in the 1890s.

Above the main street, Highfield Road had been developed in 1854, out of what had previously been just a country lane. It now formed the southern limit of the town. Below it, the early nineteenth-century terraces were partly engulfed in later buildings, including Oxford Street (now Oxford Grove) cut through from the High Street in about 1872. Hillsborough Terrace (Fig. 11) still stood in isolation, although just to the east of it building was about to start on the Chambercombe Park Estate.

FIG. 11
Hillsborough Terrace, 1864. (Courtesy WCSL).

PLATE 1
Torrs Park from Holy Trinity churchyard. The houses in the foreground are W. C. Oliver's of the early 1880s; those behind are c. 1890 by an unknown architect.

PLATE 2
The 'George and Dragon', Fore Street. One of the few pre-1700 buildings to have survived.

PLATE 3
Early or mid seventeenth-century panelled door and carved door frame at the 'George and Dragon', Fore Street.

PLATE 4
The Royal Britannia Hotel, Broad Street. Early nineteenth-century harbour front building, unusually elaborate for Ilfracombe in having bow windows.

PLATE 5
Runnamede House, Runnacleave Road. A Gothic villa of the 1840s.

PLATE 6
Nos. 8 and 9 Northfield Road. A pair of mid nineteenth-century houses with original shop fronts.

PLATE 7
Oxford Grove. Terrace houses by W. H. Gould, 1872.

PLATE 8
Seven Hills and Abbeydale (originally Sunnyside), a pair of semi-detached houses designed by W. H. Gould, 1876. An asymmetrical design with different bay windows and an angle turret at Seven Hills.

PLATE 9
The former Congregational Church (now a community centre), High Street. Remodelled in the early 1880s, probably by W. H. Gould, who designed the adjacent Sunday school (gate visible to right) in 1884.

PLATE 10
The Berkeley Hotel, Wilder Road. Built by W. M. Robbins as the Belgrave Hotel in 1884.

PLATE 11

Brookdale Lodge, Brookdale Avenue (1881), with 17–18 Church Road (1880) in the background. W. M. Robbins's own house (note the iron finial on the roof) and a pair of his Gothic semi-detached speculative houses.

PLATE 12

St Martins (originally Roslyn Hoe), Torrs Park, by W. M. Robbins c. 1880. One of the best houses in the group, its woodland background is now marred by late twentieth-century houses.

PLATES 13 AND 14

Nos. 6 and 7 Brookdale Avenue. About 1883 by W. M. Robbins. The houses are exceptionally elaborate for this street; most look like their plainer neighbour to the left.

PLATE 15

Northcote Buildings, Church Street, a terrace of houses and shops by W. M. Robbins, 1880. Polychrome brick Gothic; the nearest house (Venners) retains its original shop front.

PLATE 16

Beaconsfield Terrace, Wilder Road. Artisans and workmen's houses of 1880, probably by W. M. Robbins.

PLATE 17
No. 17 Wilder Road. A Gothic shop front of about 1880, probably by W. M. Robbins.

PLATE 18
Wilderbrook Nursing Home, Torrs Park. Originally a private house designed by W. C. Oliver, 1882. Note the carefully studied timber-framed gables, an advanced feature for this date.

PLATE 19
Stoneleigh and Gloucester Hotels, Wilder Road. Originally a terrace of four houses designed in the 'Marland brick' style by W. H. Gould, 1886. Note the typical iron balconies; the adjoining house (nearest the camera) shows one in close-up.

PLATE 20
The Lamb Inn (Hotel), High Street. 1893 by Charles Vellacott, builder. A typical piece of bay-windowed shopping-street architecture of the 1890s.

PLATE 21
Nos. 11–23 Broad Park Avenue. Marland brick terrace of the late 1890s; the upper storeys have round-arched panels filled with patterned red and cream brick. Note the garden walls and gate-piers topped with quartz blocks.

PLATE 22
No. 4 Broad Park Avenue. 1897 by Allen T. Hussell. Semi-detached house with cream and red brick front, patterned, slate-hung gable-end.

PLATE 23
Nos. 1 and 2 Church Street and 70 High Street. A terrace of Dutch-gabled houses dated 1906.

—4—
THE BUILDINGS

Although population statistics and plans are essential for understanding the phenomenal growth of late Victorian Ilfracombe, the sharpest impression of the town at that period comes from its architecture. The final burst of building in the central areas took place in the twenty-five years before the First World War, and since then remarkably little has changed. The grandest Victorian building, the Ilfracombe Hotel, has been demolished, and the second grandest, the Victoria Pavilion, rebuilt. Others have been altered, some mutilated, and new houses have been built in spaces that the Victorians wisely left open. Yet overall, total rebuildings have been rare and late Victorian architecture continues to dominate the townscape.

The extent of the change brought about by the later Victorians is best understood by looking briefly at the few earlier buildings that still exist. Those that survive from before 1700 are modest structures, reflecting Ilfracombe's status as a minor market town. The medieval parish church is small by comparison with other town churches, while the houses are rural in style, without the timber-framed gabled fronts that characterize their counterparts in Exeter, Dartmouth and Totnes and which can be found even in towns as small as Cullompton and Great Torrington. The 'George and Dragon' in Fore Street is a good example (Plates 2 and 3): low, two-storeyed, with an early or mid seventeenth-century panelled door in a moulded frame. The

Wellington in the High Street is similar, though more altered, as is probably 47 High Street, behind a late nineteenth-century re-fronting.

Truly urban houses do not seem to have come in until the beginning of the eighteenth century. The harbour area still has a few examples, like 8-9 Broad Street and 58-59 Fore Street. They have tall, narrow fronts in the London terrace-house style with such details as keystones to the window-arches and moulded cornices; unfortunately the stone and brick fronts have been painted. Only the Manor House in Quayfield Road, built for the Bourchier Wreys, lords of the manor, has any pretensions to grandeur. Yet even this looks modest by comparison with the 1690s houses in Bridgeland Street, Bideford, or with Palmer House, Great Torrington, of 1752.

It was not until the beginning of the nineteenth century that urban architecture on a large scale came to Ilfracombe, mostly in the form of simple stuccoed buildings in classical style. A number of these can still be seen in the High Street, Fore Street and around the harbour, as well as in Horne Lane, Portland Street and St Brannock's Road. Rarely do they run to more decoration than doorcases with columns, patterned iron balconies and occasionally pilasters in the upper storeys. Fronts are usually flat; the Royal Britannia Hotel in Broad Street is unusual in having three-storeyed bow windows on its harbour front (Plate 4). Even the great terraces are plain, with the addition only of pedimented centrepieces at Adelaide and Hillsborough. There is a marked contrast with places like Brighton and Torquay, and the journalist's description of the Ilfracombe terraces in 1856 as 'factory-like lines of building' is easily understandable.

Early in Victoria's reign, certainly by the mid 1840s, less austere buildings began to appear. There were Gothic villas like Runnamede in Runnacleave Road (Plate 5) and The Gables in Belmont Road. Classical houses tended to be rather more detailed: 1-5 Montpelier Road and 8-9 Northfield

Road (Plate 6), for example, have round-headed upper-storey windows and gabled dormers to match; at Northfield Road the windows are sub-divided to contain recessed, paired sashes which also have round heads. Bay windows come in, as in the upper storeys of the Victoria Hotel in High Street. At Wildersmouth Villa, in Marine Place, the facade has three square bays with Tudor-style mullioned-and-transomed windows in the ground storey, surmounted in the second storey by shallower bays with round-arched lights and classical pediments.

From about 1860 Italian influences produced still more exuberant detail. The Town Hall, built in that year with attached columns on all three storeys of its narrow stone facade, must originally have stood out from its contemporaries in the High Street. In Torrs Park the earliest group of villas, still stuccoed, had heavy porches with Italianate doorways and windows (Fig. 12).

FIG. 12
A view across Ilfracombe from the Torrs c. 1872. In the foreground are the earliest group of Torrs Park houses before the major expansion of the 1880s. (Courtesy WCSL).

—5—
ILFRACOMBE AND THE GOTHIC REVIVAL

Yet, despite these moves towards greater elaboration, nothing can have prepared the town for the Ilfracombe Hotel (Fig. 13 and page 10), built by a London architect* in 1867. Quite apart from being a major hotel by national standards (it had 210 rooms), its style was full-blown Gothic, carried out in yellow brick with red-brick and stone details. Completing it all, no doubt to provide a Continental flavour, were French Renaissance pavilion roofs, tall enough to contain two extra floors.

Gothic Revival architecture was not new to Ilfracombe. Even discounting the frothy villas of the 1840s there was already the seriously Gothic church of St Philip and St James, built by John Hayward of Exeter in 1856 (Fig. 14). But this was in plain stone, and anyway churches were expected to be Gothic. At Tiverton in 1854-6 the church of St Peter, West Exe, had been designed in Gothic, after which the new approach-road to it was promptly lined with Georgian-style houses. What was new in Ilfracombe was non-ecclesiastical building in polychrome brick and stone, and in this respect the town was now among the leaders of architectural fashion.

* M.C.W. Horne, according to a local newspaper quoted by Lois Lamplugh. B. Cherry and N. Pevsner's *Devon* (1989), in the Buildings of England series, prefers John Hayward of Exeter on stylistic grounds.

FIG. 13
An engraving of the Ilfracombe Hotel in 1868, a year after its completion. It was demolished in 1976. (From an engraving by Gadsby 24 Views of Ilfracombe, *courtesy WCSL).*

FIG. 14
A view from Capstone Hill c. 1900. In the left foreground is the church of St Philip and St James (John Hayward, 1856); on the hillside behind, Hillsborough and Montpelier Terraces. (Courtesy WCSL).

Once established, the new fashion took an immediate grip on the town. Classical architecture virtually ceased to be built and the rapid expansion of the 1870s, 1880s and 1890s was carried out almost entirely in Gothic or early Renaissance styles. Moreover, although it was predominantly speculative building, it was high-quality work of its kind. The aim was to draw people into this hitherto remote corner of Devon, either as holiday visitors or residents, and that perhaps accounts for its slightly theatrical character.

—6—
GOTHIC REVIVAL ARCHITECTS

Although the Ilfracombe Hotel had been designed by an outsider, subsequent building was mainly the work of local people, either born in the Ilfracombe district (to judge from their surnames) or attracted by the building boom to set up business in the town. The one exception was **W.C.Oliver** (c. 1833-1913), a leading Barnstaple architect whose name appears in the Ilfracombe Local Board of Health minute book as early as 1869. He designed the new post office at 41-42 High Street (now converted to shops) in cream-brick Gothic with red-brick and stone details: not much of a place compared with the hotel, but striking evidence of how quickly the new fashion caught on for smaller buildings.

The first known Gothic Revival architect to set up an office in Ilfracombe was **J.H.('Harry') Huxtable**. He was the only member of his profession listed in the town by Morris's directory for 1870 and was well enough regarded to be chosen to design the extension to the Ilfracombe Hotel in 1871. His commissions included buildings in the High Street, Torrs Park and at 1-4 Somers Crescent, the latter's buff-brick and stone fronts regrettably now painted. A fellow-architect, A.T.Hussell, writing in 1937, particularly admired his facade at 35 High Street (c.1874). It was in early English Gothic, of squared light-green local stone with dressings of Portland stone; the windows (shown in an old photograph of the

Fig. 15
A coach waits outside the Royal Clarence Hotel in the High Street c. 1890. The next house along, No. 35, by J. H. Huxtable c. 1874, was particularly admired by Allen T. Hussell as an example of mid-Victorian Gothic. (Courtesy WCSL).

Royal Clarence next door, Fig. 15) had pointed arches, those in the second storey with pillars of polished red granite. This facade, like others in the town, has now been rendered and its character wholly destroyed. It is sad to think how easily Victorian Ilfracombe could be ruined if this practice became more widespread.

By the time Harrod's directory of 1878 was compiled, Huxtable had gone. The Ilfracombe architects were now W.H.Gould and W.M.Robbins, both thorough-going Gothicists designing in polychrome brick and stone. These two, along with W.C.Oliver who worked in the town again in the 1880s, seem to have virtually transformed the architectural character of Ilfracombe in the 1870s and 1880s.

W.H.Gould (c. 1849-1937), was apparently a local man, though unrelated to R.D. Gould, the distinguished Barnstaple architect of the mid nineteenth century. He was a typically versatile Victorian figure, described in Harrod's directory of 1878 as an architect and surveyor, timber, deal and slate merchant, agent for Farmer & Co.'s chemical manures and the Phoenix Fire Co. White's directory for the same year adds that he was also a dealer in sanitary pipes and a lime burner. In the late 1880s and early 1890s he became part-time surveyor to the Local Board of Health, and for thirty years from the late 1880s he was proprietor of the Collingwood Hotel in Wilder Road.

His first known commission was to design buildings in Oxford Grove (Plate 7), newly cut through in 1872. The blocks on the two High Street corners were his, including the clock tower, and also the Oxford Hall (now occupied by the Salvation Army) on the right-hand side going up. A.T.Hussell, who had been his pupil, thought this one of his best works, but today perhaps the greatest impact is made by his terrace which runs up the whole left side of the street: a remarkably varied collection of twenty-two narrow-fronted houses, all in polychrome brick, patterned coloured tiles and stone, and all, of course, in Gothic. The architect's own office was at No. 6.

Away from the High Street, Gould's designs included a pair of semi-detached villas in Torrs Park: Seven Hills and Abbeydale of 1876 (Plate 8). These are in yellow brick decorated with red and black brick, the bay windows having Gothic details in stone. At the right-hand end of Seven Hills, in an asymmetrical position typical of the Gothic Revival, is an octagonal angle-turret with a tall pointed roof covered with patterned slates of two different colours. On one side of it is a tiny gabled dormer window (known in medievalists' jargon as a lucarne) and at the top a scrolled iron finial.

Gould's most important work in the town, however, was the Victoria Pavilion of 1888 (Fig. 16 – see also Fig. 10), a glass and iron structure in the tradition of the large conservatories, and also, of course, of the Crystal Palace in London, built in the mid nineteenth century. He was a leading Methodist and seems to have been the automatic choice for designing non-conformist churches; the Baptist Church in High Street (1891), the Methodist Church in Wilder Road (1899-1900), possibly the Congregational Church in High Street (early 1880s, now a community centre, Plate 9) and certainly its adjacent Sunday school (1884). Outside Ilfracombe he was responsible for the Methodist Church at Mortehoe (1878).

W.M.Robbins is not mentioned in the town before 1878 and vanishes equally abruptly after 1884. In that period, however, he put up at least sixteen to eighteen buildings and groups of buildings; these included eight or nine villas in Torrs Park, the whole south-east side of Brookdale Avenue, the Royal Clarence and Belgrave Hotels (the latter now re-named the Berkeley), and probably Beaconsfield Terrace in Wilder Road. He appears to be unknown as an

FIG. 16
A splendid view, c. 1895, of W. H. Gould's Victoria Pavilion (Courtesy WCSL).

architect anywhere else, yet came to Ilfracombe as an established figure; in 1881 he was in a position to purchase Bloody Field, on which Brookdale Avenue now stands, for the then quite considerable sum of £2650.

Robbins was less inclined to Gothic fantasy than Gould. He used more Renaissance details, particularly pavilion roofs, and his facades were nearly always symmetrical. Although he, too, used a lot of polychrome brick, he sometimes also produced a more rugged effect by using rough-faced stone rubble with brick dressings. The Berkeley Hotel (1884) shows him at his most imposing: a sort of French Renaissance chateau in cream brick with quite ordinary Gothic detail in red brick and stone (Plate 10). In the centre, over the main entrance, a tall, square, windowed projection rises above the roof-line, where it has a fully glazed top storey and a steep flat-topped roof, originally surmounted by an ornamental iron railing. At either end of the facade is a turret-like octagonal bay window, linked to the centre by galleries, its tall roof almost invisible under a cluster of dormers. Robbins's facade to the Royal Clarence Hotel (c. 1881), by contrast, is almost flat, as suits its position in the High Street (see Fig. 15). There are just two small bay windows; the main decorative effect is provided by a series of iron balconies and a parapet of almost oriental character.

Brookdale Lodge in Brookdale Avenue, the house that Robbins built for himself in 1881, shows him in quite a different light (Plate 11). This building, in red brick with just a touch of cream brick in the Gothic window-arches, is wholly asymmetrical, influenced no doubt by the new interest in vernacular architecture. Its best feature is a triangular bay window looking down Wilder Road, the upper storey a six-sided open wooden gallery. But, as with so many Ilfracombe buildings, a lot of the pleasure in looking at it comes from the details: a coloured-glass window and a terracotta panel on the Church Road side, a pair of fantastic iron finials on the roof.

Robbins's villas in Torrs Park display still more versatility of style. Those at the eastern end, Royston/Grangewood and Rose Garth/Carden (1879) are quite modest exercises in polychrome brick Gothic. At the western end, however, the Excelsior (originally a semi-detached pair) and St Martins (Plate 12) are quite outstanding. The Excelsior, built of stone rubble with red and yellow-brick dressings, has a large pair of flanking gabled wings, their apexes filled with the newly-fashionable timber-framing. The centre, however, instead of being at a lower level in the traditional medieval manner, rises above the gables to finish in a steep French-style roof, in the centre of which is a dormer window, now altered but shown in the architect's original drawing with exposed timber-framing. At either end are further wings facing sideways, their roofs with half-hipped overhanging gables, deeply coved on the underside. St Martins is quite different: a delicate design in red brick, with details in black brick, red terracotta and stone. It has two steep, closely-set gables, the windows of which are set in tall yellow-brick recesses with pointed arches, while the gables are finished with French-style patterned bargeboards. In the centre the projecting entrance-porch is surmounted by a fully-glazed, semi-octagonal bay window with a pointed roof.

Robbins's smaller semi-detached houses, though of course more modest in detail, display an equal range of invention: 17-18 and 19-20 Church Road (1880) are twin-gabled pairs in rough-faced stone with details in dressed stone and red and yellow brick (Plate 11). Though built to the same basic design, they differ significantly in some features. Nos. 17-18 have two-storeyed bay windows with trefoiled heads to the lights and a battlemented parapet at the top: Nos. 19-20 have this kind of bay only in the ground storey, the upper storey having triangular bays with Tudor-style mullions and curved Regency roofs. Nos. 17-18 have patterned bargeboards: Nos. 19-20 have plain ones. The houses round the corner in Brookdale Avenue are mostly more workaday designs; A. T.

Hussell described them as 'designed in the office of Mr Robbins'. Nos. 6-7 (Plates 13 and 14), however, are transformed by the addition of Gothic bay windows to otherwise simple red-brick houses with bands of yellow brick. The bays are of three storeys, rising through the gables to half-hipped roofs. Built of wood with cast-iron Gothic shafts at the corners and between the lights, the window-heads in the second and third storeys are decorated with quatrefoils and circles, and above these are deep, bracketed cornices with crestings of small iron flowers.

The best of Robbins's buildings in the main street are Nos. 7-10 Church Street (Northcote Buildings, Plate 15), a polychrome brick terrace of shops and houses with Gothicized Venetian windows. He was probably responsible also for Beaconsfield Terrace in Wilder Road (Plate 16). This is a more austere design in stone rubble and cream brick, but beautifully detailed for a row of artisans' dwellings; among the occupants in 1881 were a plumber, a painter, a mason, a general labourer, a railway clerk and a railway porter. Probably the attractive shop front at No. 17 (adjoining the end of the terrace, facing Bradwell Road) belonged to the same development (Plate 17).

W. C. Oliver returned to work in the town in the early 1880s. He did at least one building in the High Street (Nos. 110-112), but principally he was involved in the extension of Torrs Park, which had ended the 1860s with just one short row of villas at the east end. According to his obituary in the *North Devon Journal* he was responsible for laying out the Park. Certainly the part of it developed by Shapland and Petter of Barnstaple, whose architect he was, included the building of Osborne Road leading from Torrs Park to the parish church. His architectural contribution, however, seems to have been limited to a row of seven distinctive villas (four of them semi-detached) on the south side, from Parkroyd to Torrsvale, together with Westwell Hall which stands apart in a slip-road off the north side (Fig. 17). All eight houses are in Oliver's favourite cream-coloured Marland brick with dressings of red brick and stone. Their style can best be described as monumental, particularly when viewed from the parish church across the West Wilder valley (see Plate 1). At first sight they seem to be all gables and three or four-storeyed bay windows, but although there is a rather stark quality about them there is also a lot of good detail. Several have timber-framing in the gables, an advanced feature for this date; unlike Robbins's framing it is carefully studied, with square and round-headed panels, arch-bracing and herringbone-pattern (Plate 18). Some houses have Gothic tracery with coloured glass; others have ornate wooden balconies on the rear elevations, while Glen Tor and Torrsvale have good conservatories on the side-walls. Westwell Hall has an imposing entrance-porch and, at the entrance to the drive, elaborate iron gates filled with a mixture of classical and Gothic motifs and surmounted by a pair of lamps (see page 8).

FIG. 17 (overleaf)
Plans for a house in Torrs Park by W. C. Oliver. The design was used for two houses, now the Wilderbrook Nursing Home annexe, and the Southcliffe Hotel. R. Lake, whose signature appears on the drawings, was chairman of the local authority, then known as the Ilfracombe Local Board of Health. (Courtesy North Devon Record Office).

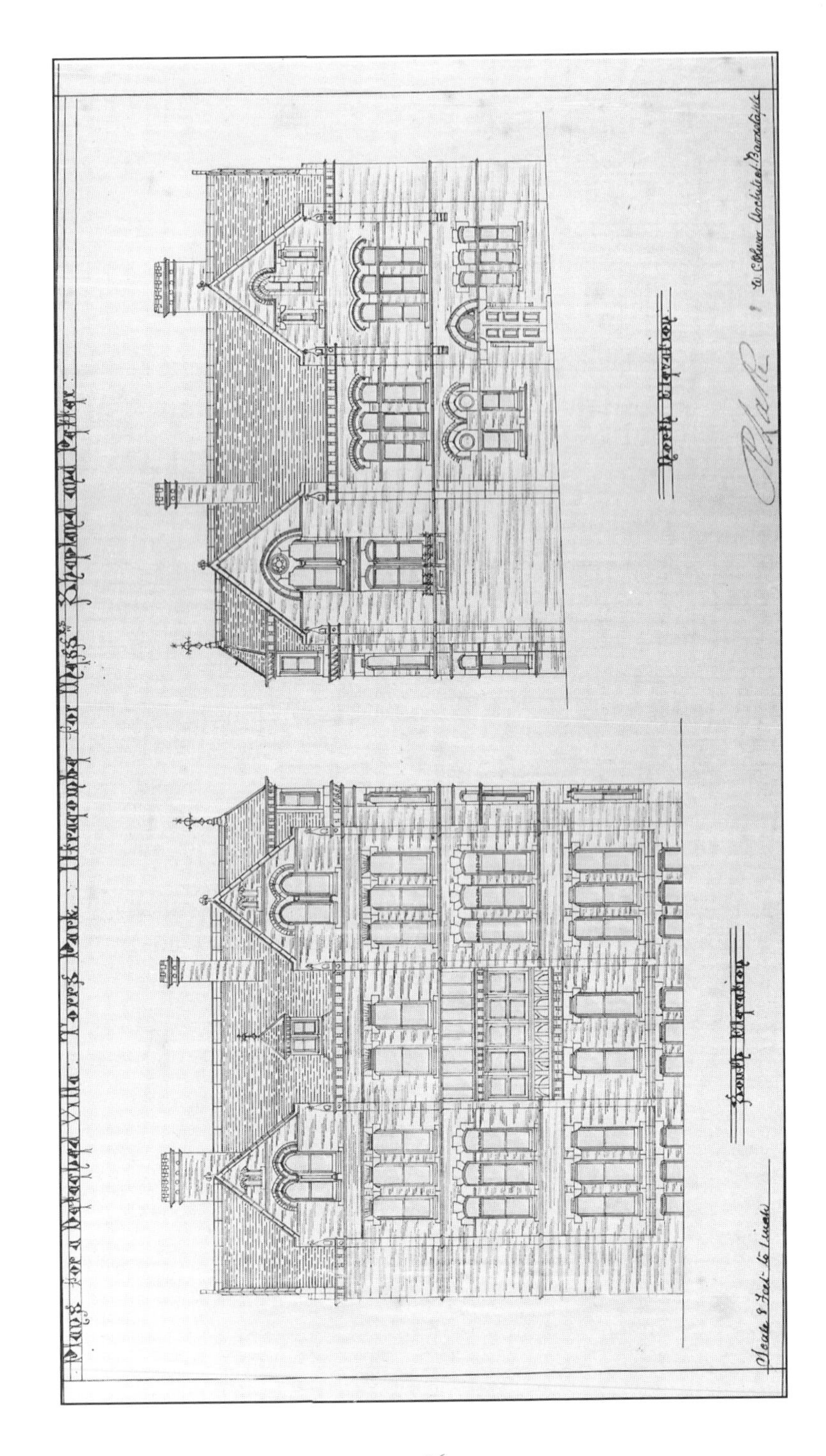
Plans for a Detached Villa 'Torrs Park,' Ilfracombe for Messrs Shapland and Petter
North Elevation
South Elevation
Scale 8 Feet to 1 inch
W. C. Oliver Architect Barnstaple

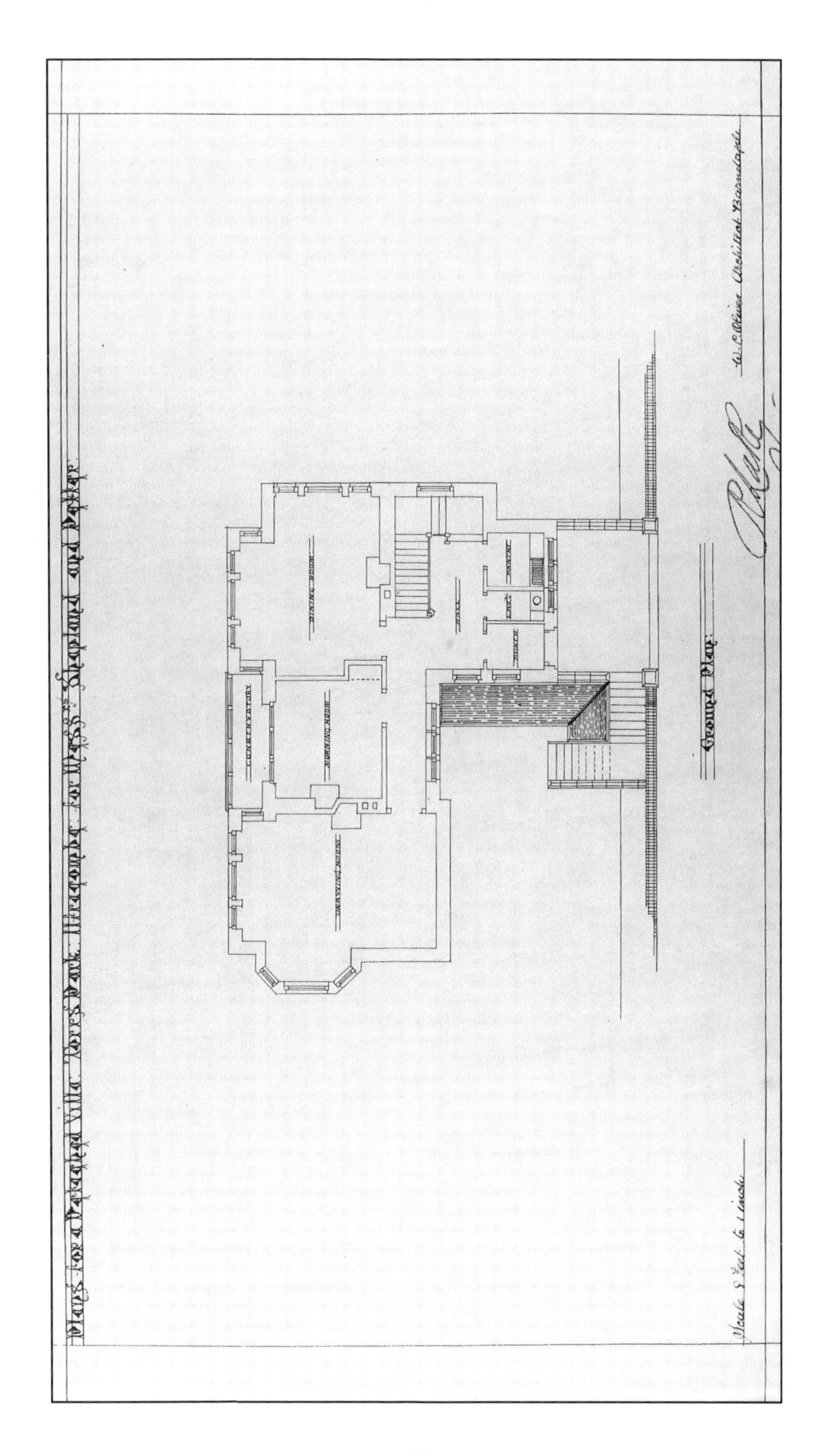
Plans for a Detached Villa Torrs Park Ilfracombe for Messrs Shapland and Petter
Dining Room
Morning Room
Drawing Room
Conservatory
Ground Plan
W. C. Oliver Architect Barnstaple
Scale 8 feet to 1 inch

—7— ARCHITECTS OF THE LATE 1880S AND EARLY 1890S

Towards the end of the 1880s Ilfracombe architecture changed considerably. Except for W. H. Gould, the leading figures of the Gothic Revival had gone. Polychrome brick was still in fashion, but it was now used with more restraint. Cream-coloured Marland brick predominated, with red brick used for window-arches and for simple decorative bands and wall-patterns. The usual style was austere, owing much more to the early Renaissance than to the Gothic. However, patterned coloured glass was still as popular and a note of gaiety was added by the numerous iron balconies, sometimes decorating as many as three storeys in the boarding-houses. The balconies seem to have been limited to two or three patterns, probably derived from Regency originals. Another extravagant feature introduced at this time was the pair of gate piers piled high with a miniature rockery of white quartz blocks. 'The Quarry' in Torrs Park Road has a good example, complete with original wooden gates.

W. H. Gould was now designing in the new 'Marland brick' style. A terrace of four houses in Wilder Road (now the Stoneleigh and Gloucester Hotels) was almost certainly built by him in 1886 (Plate 19); the gable-end is distinguished by a large chimney in panelled red brick. For some of his major works, however, he used a rather stark Gothic, with rough-faced brown-stone walling and dressings of cream brick. The former Runnacleave Hotel (1891) is among these, unfortunately now without the long glazed passage, a miniature version of the Victoria Pavilion, that formerly linked it to Wilder Road. The Granville Hotel was built in a similar style in the same year and was probably also Gould's work. This, however, is a mock castle, particularly effective when seen from Capstone Hill with the cliff-face dropping steeply down to the sea in front of it. A few of the more romantic details have gone since 1891, but it is still one of the most striking buildings in the town.

One of the grandest examples of the 'Marland brick' style is **Joseph Yeardye's** masonic hall of 1888 at 141-144 High Street (now a discount store). Yeardye, who lived in Ilfracombe, seems to have been at the beginning of his career in the town at this time. He used the wooden bay windows that often went with High Street buildings in the 1890s, decorated only with simple panels and light cornices, but in the centre is a five-light Romanesque window in stone. Presumably this was intended to light the masons' meeting room, for at either end is a stone plaque which until recently bore the shadow of the masonic symbol.

Less ambitious versions of the style were subsequently put up by men who are described as builders in the directories, but whose names appear in the 'architect' column of the Local Board of Health planning register. Such were **Charles Vellacott**, builder and contractor, and **F. J. Reed**, builder and undertaker. Vellacott was named in the register as architect of the Lamb Hotel (Plate 20) in High Street (1893). It has a pair of wooden bay windows like those in Yeardye's Masonic Hall, except that the first-floor windows have transom-lights of patterned, coloured glass. In the centre is a recess with a round red-brick arch containing the name and date of the building, the latter in its own frame with a red-brick lugged apron below and a triangular pediment above. A rather similar house at 118-119 High Street (architect unknown) has panels of patterned red terracotta between the bays. F J Reed was responsible for a more modest version of the design at 147 High Street. This has only a rendered front, but nearly all of it is taken up by a bay window rising through all three upper storeys. The transom-lights contain patterned coloured glass and the upper sashes have margin-panes, another common feature of the late nineteenth century.

Vellacott was also responsible for 13-18 St Brannock's Road (1895), a fine terrace in similar style, marking the entrance to the town centre on the Braunton side. These six houses are of cream brick with arches and bands of red brick, each front dominated by a wooden bay window with a prominent bracketed cornice at first-floor level; between the brackets, in a detail typical of these seemingly simple buildings, are small quatrefoils. Nos. 1-14 Langleigh Road (1893: architect unknown) are a slightly more imposing version of the same design, as befits a terrace which faces Torrs Park across the West Wilder valley. Here the bays are simpler, but the brickwork between them has decorated red-terracotta bands at first-floor level. Instead of the relatively plain gabled dormers in St Brannock's Road, the ones here have two-light round-arched windows, the lights separated by a column with moulded capital and base. At No. 1 is a beautifully-made red-terracotta plaque moulded with the inscription: '18 LANGLEIGH TERRACE 93'.

—8—

THE LATE 1890S AND EARLY TWENTIETH CENTURY

The late 1890s saw the return of more romantic architectural styles, particularly in Broad Park Avenue, laid out in 1897 (Plate 21). This is perhaps the most exciting suburban street in Ilfracombe, with designs ranging from polychrome Gothic to tile and slate-hung vernacular revival. The same cream brick and rough-faced stone are used, but with bargeboarded gables, wooden balconies and inset panels of red brick. Not only the gate piers, but the whole of the front garden walls are topped with quartz blocks. The vernacular revival houses mostly have patterned red tile-hanging, a south-eastern fashion wholly alien to the Devon building tradition, although there are two more appropriate slate-hung examples at the lower end. The best of the latter (No. 1) is probably by F. J. Reed, banded with blue and gilt slate in diamond and fish-scale patterns.

Across the road at Nos. 2-6 **Allen T. Hussell** also used slate-hanging on his gable-walls (Plate 22). It may be that he designed other buildings in the street; the inset Gothic panels at Nos. 14-16 and 22 are reminiscent of the 1870s style of W. H. Gould, whose pupil he had been. Hussell (born 1870) was a native of Ilfracombe, and as versatile as his master, although in a different way. He was a pianist and composer, and in 1912 was engaged to play on a cruise ship to the Amazon. After the First World War he composed music for several popular songs, including 'Coachman Sam' with its refrain 'On the Lynton road in the morning'. He was also an architectural historian; in 1909 he published a book on *North Devon Churches* and in 1937 a series of articles on Ilfracombe buildings in the *Ilfracombe Chronicle*. The latter is a remarkable assessment of the town's Victorian architecture by one who had been closely involved in its later period.

Elsewhere in the town there was a minor enthusiasm for Dutch gables. The best of them are at 1-2 Church Street and 70 High Street (1906): fairly plain red and cream brick with canted wooden bay windows, topped with fantastic scrolled, pedimented and finialed stone gables (Plate 23). The present Post Office building and, at the far end of the town, 132 High Street, are plainer examples of the same style. Perhaps the last fling of the fantasy styles was the Gaiety Theatre (c. 1910) on the Promenade. Its ground storey is now lost in an amusement arcade and shops, but the upper storey remains more or less intact. Three great semi-circular windows with tall keystones occupy the main front, each with a glazed door in the middle, that in the centre framed with decorative ironwork (now mostly gone) and rising through the semi-circle to finish in a secondary round arch. At the left end is a small angle-turret with a conical roof, its eaves swept out to protect a frieze of moulded plasterwork.

In 1913 Allen Hussell submitted to the Urban District Council designs for Westaway, a combined house and dentist's surgery which still stands next to the Tunnels Baths. It has lost a little of its detail, but it remains what it was always intended to be, a simple detached house in one of the plainest of the suburban styles that were to become popular in the 1920s and 1930s. The contrast between this and Hussell's vernacular designs for Broad Park Avenue, sixteen years earlier, seems to mark the end of an era for Ilfracombe architecture.

By the 1920s Ilfracombe was ceasing to be a fashionable resort; its few new buildings, such as the Pavilion Theatre of

1925, reflect its decline. Although spared the large-scale developments of the 1960s to 1980s, its older buildings have often been marred by cheap, flat-roofed extensions and their brickwork and masonry painted or rendered. It is to be hoped that historic buildings legislation will prove adequate to protect the best mid-to-late Victorian town in Devon from further damage.

SOURCES

The background material for this book has been drawn mostly from Bruce May's 'The Rise of Ilfracombe as a Seaside Resort in the Nineteenth and Early Twentieth Centuries' (in *Exeter Papers in Economic History*, No. 13, University of Exeter, 1980), and from Lois Lamplugh's *A History of Ilfracombe* (1984). Other sources have been directories and guidebooks, including E.D. Bourdillon's manuscript 'Narrative of a Three Weeks Tour in the Western Counties' (1834), which is in Totnes Museum.

Information on building dates and architects comes mainly from the minute-books of the Ilfracombe Local Board of Health and from its register of plans, the latter starting in 1880 and including many original plans and elevations. The minute books and about ten per cent of the plans are in the North Devon Record Office; a microfilm of the complete register is held by the Planning Department of North Devon District Council. The files of the *Ilfracombe Chronicle* (now in Ilfracombe Museum) have also been useful, expecially Allen T. Hussell's series of articles on Ilfracombe architecture, published between 28 May and 17 September 1937. I am grateful to Martin Reardon of the former Ilfracombe Community Project for drawing my attention to this and other material.

The best published collection of drawings and photographs of Old Ilfracombe is in Glenn K. Horridge's *Ilfracombe, A Pictorial Record* (1986).